Livewire Classics

.R ARTHUR CONAN DOYLE'S

The Speckled Band

Peter Leigh

Published in association with The Basic Skills Agency

Hodder & Stoughton
A MEMBER OF THE HODDER HEADLINE GROUP

Acknowledgements
Cover: Fred van Deelen
Illustrations: Linda Clark
Photograph: Hulton Getty

Every effort has been made to trace copyright holders of material reproduced in this book. Any rights not acknowledged will be acknowledged in subsequent printings if notice is given to the publisher.

Orders; please contact Bookpoint Ltd, 39 Milton Park, Abingdon, Oxon OX14 4TD. Telephone: (44) 01235 400414, Fax: (44) 01235 400454. Lines are open from 9.00–6.00, Monday to Saturday, with a 24 hour message answering service.
Email address: orders@bookpoint.co.uk

British Library Cataloguing in Publication Data
A catalogue record for this title is available from the British Library

ISBN 0 340 77464 9

First published 2000
Impression number 10 9 8 7 6 5 4 3 2 1
Year   2005 2004 2003 2002 2001 2000

Typeset by GreenGate Publishing Services, Tonbridge, Kent.
Printed in Great Britain for Hodder and Stoughton Educational, a division of Hodder Headline Plc, 338 Euston Road, London NW1 3BH, by Redwood Books Ltd, Trowbridge, Wilts

About the author

Conan Doyle wrote hundreds of stories.
He was one of the most popular writers
of all time.
But he is best known for one man –
the famous detective **Sherlock Holmes**.

About the story

All the stories about Sherlock Holmes
are told by his friend Doctor Watson.

In this story they are having breakfast
when there is a knock at the door.

Their visitor is a lady.

I

'Come in,' said Holmes.
'My name is Sherlock Holmes.'
He turned to me.
'And this is Doctor Watson.'

She was dressed in black,
and wore a heavy veil.

'Draw up to the fire,' he said.
'Shall I order you a cup of hot coffee?
For I see you are shivering.'

'It is not cold
which makes me shiver,'
said the lady in a low voice.

'What then?'

'It is fear, Mr Holmes!
It is terror!'

She lifted her veil.
She was a young woman,
but her face was drawn and grey,
and her eyes were frightened.

'Have no fear,' said Holmes.
'We shall soon set matters right.
You have come by train, I see.
You must have started early,
because you have had a long drive
in a dog-cart
before you reached the station.'

The lady started,
and looked amazed.

This is why Sherlock Holmes is famous – he sees things that everyone else misses.

dog-cart – a horse and cart, used like a taxi

'There is no mystery, my dear madam,'
said Holmes.
'I can see a return ticket in your glove.
There is mud on your jacket in seven places.
The marks are fresh.
Only a dog-cart throws up mud like that.'

'You are right –
I left early this morning to come to you.
Sir, I can stand the strain no longer.
I shall go mad if it carries on.
And yet I can tell no-one –
my fears will seem silly to someone else.
So I have no-one to turn to.'

'Tell me everything.'

'My name is Helen Stoner.
I live with my stepfather, Doctor Roylott.
My mother was a rich lady.
When she died
she left her money to my stepfather.
But there was one condition.
If my sister or I got married,
then the money would come to us.

After our mother died,
a change came over our stepfather.
He became violent and bad-tempered.
He kept wild animals in the house.
My poor sister felt it most.
She was only thirty at the time of her death,
but she had already begun to go grey.'

'Your sister is dead then?'

'She died just two years ago.
It is of her death
that I wish to speak to you.
She got engaged to be married.
My stepfather did not object.
But two weeks later
the terrible event happened
that is seared into my memory.'

seared – burnt

Holmes leant forward in his chair.

'Our house is very old,
and we live in one part of it.
There are three bedrooms on the ground floor –
my stepfather's, my sister's, and my own.
There is no door between these bedrooms.
They each have a door onto the passage.
The windows open out onto the lawn.
Is that clear?'

'Yes,' said Holmes.

'That night my stepfather went to bed early.
My sister could not sleep
because of the smell of his strong cigars.
So she came into my room.
We sat chatting for some time.
"Tell me Helen," she said,
"have you ever heard anyone whistle
in the dead of the night?"

"Never," I said.

"Because during the last few nights
I have always heard a low, clear whistle
about three in the morning.
I am a light sleeper,
and it has woken me up.
I cannot tell where it came from –
perhaps from the next room,
or perhaps from the lawn.
I thought I would just ask you
whether you had heard it."

"No, I have not.
But I sleep more heavily than you."

"Well, it is no great matter at any rate."

She smiled back at me,
closed my door,
and a few moments later
I heard her key turn in the lock.'

'Indeed?' said Holmes.
'Did you always lock
yourselves in at night?'

'Always!'

'And why?'

'Remember my stepfather
keeps wild animals.
We didn't feel safe
unless our doors were locked.'

'Quite so. Please carry on.'

'I could not sleep that night.
My sister and I were twins, and very close.
It was a wild night.
The wind was howling outside,
and the rain was beating against the
windows.
Suddenly I heard a wild scream
from my sister's room.
I sprang from my bed,
and rushed into the passage.

As I opened my door,
I heard a low whistle
just as my sister had described.
A second later there was a clanging sound
as if a heavy mass of metal had fallen.

As I ran down the passage
my sister's door slowly opened.
I saw my sister appear at the doorway.
Her face was white with terror.
Her hands were groping for help,
and her whole figure was swaying to and fro.

I ran to her,
and threw my arms around her,
but at that moment her knees gave way
and she fell to the ground.
She writhed in terrible pain,
convulsed – twisted   and her limbs were dreadfully convulsed.

As I bent over her
she shrieked out,
"Oh, my God! Helen!
It was the band!
The speckled band!"

She tried to say something else,
and pointed at my stepfather's room,
but she choked on her words.

I rushed out,
shouting for my stepfather.
He came out of his room
in his dressing gown.
When he got to my sister
she was unconscious.
He poured brandy down her throat,
and sent for help to the village.
But it was no good.
She slowly sank,
and died without regaining consciousness.

Such was the dreadful end
of my beloved sister.'

'One moment,' said Holmes.
'Are you sure about this whistle
and metallic sound?
Could you swear to it?'

'I am sure I heard it.
And yet in the crash of the gale,
and the creaking of the old house,
I may have been wrong.'

'Was your sister dressed?'

'No, she was in her nightdress.
She had a matchbox in one hand,
and a dead match in the other.'

struck a light –
remember this story
was written before
there was electricity.

'Which shows she struck a light
and looked about her.
That is important.
What did the doctor say?'

'He couldn't find any cause of death.
The doors and windows were all secure.
So my sister was alone
when she met her end.
Besides,
there were no marks of violence upon her.'

'How about poison?'

'The doctor could find no sign of it.'

'How then do you think
your sister died?'

'I believe she died of pure fear,
though I don't know
what frightened her so much.'

'And what about this band?
What was it –
a speckled band?'

'I have no idea.'

'Hmm,' said Holmes.
'These are very deep waters.
Please go on.'

This is very
mysterious.

'This was two years ago,
and since then my life has been
more lonely than ever.
Until just recently,
when I met a dear man.
He has asked me to marry him.
My stepfather does not object,
and we are to be married in the spring.

9

But two days ago,
I had to move into my sister's room
because some repairs to the house were
begun.
Imagine then my terror
when in the middle of last night,
I heard the same low whistle
she had told me of.

I sprang up, and lit a lamp.
but nothing was to be seen.
I could not go back to bed.
I dressed, and as soon as it was light,
I went out, found a dog-cart
to take me to the station,
and came to see you.'

'You have done wisely,' said Holmes.
'But you have not told me all.'

'Yes, I have!'

'Miss Stoner, you have not.
You are shielding your stepfather.'

'Why, what do you mean?'

Holmes did not answer.
He leant forward
and pushed back the cuff of her sleeve.

livid spots – bruises

On her white wrist
were five livid spots,
the marks of four fingers and a thumb.

cruelly used –
treated badly

'You have been cruelly used,' said Holmes.

coultered – blushed

The lady coloured deeply,
and covered over her injured wrist.
'He is a hard man,' she said.
'He does not know his own strength.'

'Miss Stoner, we have no time to lose.
I must see the bedroom.
If we came to your house today,
could we see the room
without your stepfather knowing?'

'Yes. He said he was coming to town today.'

'Good! If you go back now,
we shall be there this afternoon.'

She rose.
'Thank you,' she said.
'My heart is so much lighter now.
I look forward to seeing you this afternoon.'

She dropped the veil over her face,
and glided from the room.

II

Holmes sat in silence for some time.
Finally he said,
'Well Watson, what do you think of that?'

'I do not know,' I said.
'It seems a dark and sinister business.'

'It is – what with a whistle,
a metallic clang, a speckled band,
and this fierce old doctor.
He would lose a lot of money
if his stepdaughters were married …
But what, in the name of the devil?'

The door suddenly crashed open.
Framed in the doorway
was a huge man.
His head nearly reached the top,
and he held a whip in his right hand.
His face was evil,
with deep-set, angry eyes.

He looked from one to the other of us.

'Which of you is Holmes?'

'That's my name, sir!
But I don't know yours,'
said Holmes quietly.

'I am Doctor Roylott.'

'Indeed, sir!
Please take a seat.'

'I will do nothing of the kind!
My stepdaughter has been here.
I have traced her.
What has she been saying to you?'

'It's a little cold for the time of year,'
said Holmes.

'What has she been saying to you?'
screamed the Doctor furiously.

'But I believe the flowers promise well.'

'Ha! You are trying to put me off.'
The Doctor stepped forward,
and shook his whip.

'I know you!
I have heard of you!
You are Holmes the meddler!'

Holmes smiled.

'Holmes the busybody!'

His smile broadened.

'Holmes the scoundrel!'

Holmes chuckled.

'Your conversation is most entertaining.
When you go out,
close the door behind you.'

'I will go when I have had my say.
Don't you dare meddle in my affairs.
I am a dangerous man.
See here!'

He stepped forward,
picked up the poker,
and bent it with his huge hands.

'See you keep out of my grip!' he snarled.
He hurled the twisted poker
into the fireplace,
and strode out of the room.

'He seems a very friendly person,' said
Holmes.
'If he had stayed I might have shown him
that I have a grip as well.'

He picked up the steel poker,
and with a sudden effort
straightened it out again.

'Fancy him having the insolence
to come here.
This makes me more determined than ever.
We must set off without delay.'

III

'I have been waiting so eagerly for you,'
said Miss Stoner.
She was in the garden
of a large country house.
We had just arrived.

'My stepfather has gone to town,
and won't be back before evening.'

'We have already met the Doctor,'
said Holmes.
He explained quickly what had happened.
Miss Stoner turned white to the lips
as she listened.

'Good heavens!' she said.
'He has followed me then?'

'So it appears.'

'He is so cunning
that I never know
when I am safe from him.'

'Then there is no time to lose.
Let us examine these rooms now!'

The house was built of stone.
There was scaffolding at one end.
No workmen were there.

Holmes stopped to look at it.

'There does not seem to be
any need for repairs.'

'There were none,' said Miss Stoner.
'It was an excuse
to move me from my room.'

'Ah,' said Holmes,
'that is significant.'

He examined the windows carefully.

'These windows are secure,' he said.
'No one could pass through.
Let us go in.'

They went into the passage.
There were three doors off it.
Holmes went straight to the middle room.
It was the one
in which Miss Stoner was sleeping –
the one in which her sister had died.

The furniture was very old.
There was a chest of drawers, a bed,
and a dressing table.

Holmes drew a chair
into the corner of the room,
and sat down silently.
His eyes travelled round and round
taking in every detail.

bell-rope – these
hung in the rooms of
rich people. When
you pulled it, a bell
rang in the servants'
room.

At last he said,
'Where does that bell-rope go to?'
He pointed to a thick bell-rope
that hung down beside the bed.

'It goes to the servant's room.'

'It looks newer than the other things.'

'Yes, it was only put there two years ago.'

'Your sister asked for it, I suppose?'

'No, I never heard of her using it.'

'How odd!
It seems very silly to put a bell-rope there.'

Holmes got up,
and walked over to the bed.

He stared at it,
and ran his eye up and down the rope.
Finally he took the rope in his hand,
and gave it a tug.

'Why, it's a dummy,' he said.

'Won't it ring?'

'No, it is not even fixed to a wire.
You can see it just hangs from a hook
above that vent.
And the vent doesn't go to outside,
but to next door.'

'How absurd!
I never noticed that before.'

'Very strange,' said Holmes.
'A bell-rope that won't pull,
and a vent that won't ventilate.
Let's go next door.'

Doctor Roylott's room was a little bigger.
There was a bed, a bookcase,
a chair against the wall,
and a large iron safe.

'What's in here?' said Holmes,
tapping the safe.

'My stepfather's papers.'

'Oh, you've seen inside then?'

'Only once, some years ago.'

'There isn't a cat in it, for example?'

'No! What a strange idea!'

'Well, look at this!'

There was a small saucer of milk
on top of the safe.

'We don't have a cat.
But my stepfather does keep wild animals.'

'Yes, but a saucer of milk will not go far.
There is just one more thing
I wish to look at.'

He bent down in front of the chair,
and examined it closely.

'Thank you,' he said, getting up,
'that is … Hallo!
Here is something interesting.'

There was a small dog-lead
hanging over the bed.
One end had been tied
to make a small loop.

'What do you make of that, Watson?'

'It's a common enough lead.
But I don't know
why it should be tied like that.'

'That is not so common, is it?
Well Miss Stoner, I have seen enough.'

He fell silent,
and paced up and down, deep in thought.
Miss Stoner and I waited.

When he spoke, his face was grim,
and his brow was dark.

'It is very important, Miss Stoner,' he said,
'that you do exactly as I say.'

'I will certainly do so.'

'It's too serious for anything else.
Your life may depend on it.'

'I am in your hands.'

'In the first place Watson and I
must spend the night in your room.'

Both Miss Stoner and I gazed at him
in astonishment.

'Yes it must be so.
Let me explain.
Pretend to be ill tonight,
and stay in your room.
When you hear your stepfather come to bed,
open your window,
and shine a light.
Watson and I will be outside.
Then quietly go back next door
to your old room.
I'm sure you can manage there
for one night.'

'Oh yes, easily.'

'Then leave the rest to us.'

'But what will you do?'

'We shall find out the cause of this noise
which has disturbed you.'

'I believe you already know.'

'Perhaps.'

'Then for pity's sake tell me.
What was the cause of my sister's death.'

'I need clearer proofs
before I speak.'

'Did she die from fright?'

'No I do not think so.
There was something else.
But now, Miss Stoner,
we must go before your stepfather returns.
Goodbye, and be brave!'

IV

Later that evening
Sherlock Holmes and I waited in the darkness
outside the house.

'Watson,' he said,
'I'm not sure
I should take you tonight.
It could be very dangerous.'

'Will I be of help?'

'Of course.'

'Then I shall certainly come.'

'That is very kind of you.'

'You speak of danger.
You must have seen more in these rooms
than I did.'

'No, I didn't see more,
but I think I may have deduced more.
You saw the same as I did.'

deduced –
understood. He has
seen the same
things as Doctor
Watson, but they
meant much more to
him.

'I saw nothing unusual except the bell-rope.
What its purpose is,
I've no idea.'

'You saw the vent?'

'Yes, but it's not that odd.
And it's very small.'

'I knew we should find a vent
before we even came to the house.'

'My dear Holmes!'

'Oh, yes I did!
Miss Stoner said
her sister could smell a cigar.
That at once suggested a vent.'

'What harm can there be in that?'

'Well, it is at least odd.
A vent is made,
a cord is hung,
and a lady who sleeps in the bed dies.
Does not that strike you?'

'I cannot see any connection.'

'Did you see anything very odd
about the bed?'

'No!'

'It was clamped to the floor.
Have you ever seen a bed
clamped like that before?'

'I cannot say that I have.'

'The lady could not move her bed.
It must always be in the same position
with the bell-rope next to it.'

'Holmes,' I cried,
'I begin to see
what you are hinting at.
We are only just in time
to stop a horrible crime.'

'Horrible enough, and …
Ah, there is our signal.'

A single bright light shone out in front of us.

Silently we passed over the lawn,
opened the window,
and crept in.

Holmes moved the lamp onto the table,
and looked around.
All was as we had seen it in the daytime.

He whispered into my ear,
so gently that I could hardly make out the
words.

'The least sound would be fatal.'

I nodded.

'We must sit without light.
He would see it through the vent.'

I nodded again.

'Do not go to sleep!
Your very life may depend on it.
Have your pistol ready
in case we should need it.
I will sit on the side of the bed,
and you in the chair.'

I took out my pistol,
and laid it on the corner of the table.

Holmes had brought a long thin cane.
He put it on the bed beside him.
Next to it he put a box of matches
and a candle.

Then he turned off the lamp,
and we were left in darkness.

How shall I ever forget that dreadful wait?
I could not hear a sound,
not even a breath.
Twelve struck, and one,
and two and three,
and still we sat waiting silently.

Suddenly there was a gleam of light
by the vent.
It went out immediately.
I heard a gentle sound of movement,
and then all was silent once more.
For half an hour
I sat with straining ears.
Then suddenly I heard another sound –
a very gentle soothing sound,
like a small jet of steam from a kettle.

The instant we heard it,
Holmes sprung from the bed.
He struck a match,
and lashed at the bell-rope
with his cane.

'You see it, Watson?' he yelled.
'You see it?'

But I saw nothing.
I heard a low, clear whistle,
but the sudden glare from the match
meant I couldn't see anything.

Holmes had stopped lashing the bell-rope,
and was gazing up at the vent.
There was then the most horrible cry
I have ever heard.

It struck cold into our hearts,
until at last it faded away.

'What can it mean?' I gasped.

'It means that it is all over,' said Holmes.
'And perhaps, after all, it is for the best.
Take your pistol,
and we shall enter Doctor Roylott's room.'

He lit the lamp,
and led the way to the corridor
into Doctor Roylott's room.

The door of the safe was open.
Beside it sat Doctor Roylott.
Across his lap was the dog-lead
we had noticed earlier.
His eyes were fixed in a dreadful, rigid stare
at the corner of the ceiling.
Round his head
he had a strange yellow band
with brownish speckles.
As we entered he made
neither sound nor motion.

'The band! The speckled band,'
whispered Holmes.

I took a step forward.
In an instant the speckled band
began to move,
and there reared up from his hair
the head of a snake.

'It's a swamp adder,' said Holmes.
'The deadliest snake in India.
He has died within ten seconds
of being bitten.
Let us put it back into its den,
and then get the police.'

As he spoke he drew the lead
from the dead man's lap,
and slipped the loop over the snake's neck.
He carried it at arm's length to the safe,
and closed the door.

Such are the true facts
of the death of Doctor Roylott.

V

Later as we travelled back, Holmes said,
'As soon as I saw the bell-rope
I thought it must be a bridge
for something to go from the vent to the bed.
I thought of a rare snake
because of the Doctor's wild pets,
and because nobody would be able
to detect the poison.

Then I thought of the whistle.
Of course he must call the snake back
before morning.
He probably trained it with the milk.
He would put it through the vent,
and it would crawl down the rope to the bed.
Anyone sleeping there would be bitten,
sooner or later.

There were marks on his chair
that showed he had been standing on it,
probably to reach the vent.
And when I saw the safe,
the saucer of milk, and the lead,
that was enough to convince me.
The clang heard by Miss Stoner
was her stepfather closing the safe door.

I heard the snake hiss,
and I instantly lit the light
and attacked it.'

'And drove it back through the vent.'

'And caused it to turn on its master
on the other side.
I had roused its snakish temper,
so that it flew upon the first person it saw.
So I am responsible
for Doctor Roylott's death,
but I cannot say that will upset me too
much.'